Isaac S. Moses

The Message of the Hour

Isaac S. Moses

The Message of the Hour

ISBN/EAN: 9783337084783

Printed in Europe, USA, Canada, Australia, Japan

Cover: Foto ©Lupo / pixelio.de

More available books at **www.hansebooks.com**

THE MESSAGE OF THE HOUR.

FOUR SERMONS

DELIVERED ON THE NEW YEARS' DAY, AND
THE DAY OF ATONEMENT, 5651—1890.

BY

ISAAC S. MOSES,

RABBI OF CONGREGATION ANSHE MAARAB.

CHICAGO, ILL.
E. RUBOVITS & BRO., PUBLISHERS.
1890.

To my venerable friend and predecessor
in the pulpit,
The Rev. Dr. Liebman Adler,
these few pages are dedicated, as a
token of love and friendship.
I. S. Moses.

THE MESSAGE OF THE HOUR.

SERMON FOR NEW YEAR'S EVE.

Text: Malachi iii. 22, 24. "Behold I send unto you Elijah, the prophet, and he shall turn the heart of the fathers to the children, and the heart of the children to the fathers."

I Kings, Chap. xvii, 1.—"And Elijah the Tishbite, who was of the inhabitants of Gilead, said to Ahab, As the Eternal the God of Israel liveth, before whom I stand, there shall not be dew nor rain these years, but according to my word.

Silently and noiselessly it has come and gone, the year just past, and with sudden step the young giant, the new year, enters upon the threshold of time, like that gaunt figure of old, who, as we read in ancient lore, often unexpected and unbidden appeared before the king and the people, exhorting, rebuking, threatening, but also advising and encouraging. It is the towering, heroic figure of the Thesbian prophet, Elijah, on whose brow the grateful memory of popular tradition has placed a crown of immortal glory, sparkling with the gems of myth and miracle, of song and story, of national ambition and lofty ideals, of undaunted courage and grim victory; of remorse, weariness and despair; of reawakened hope and undying faith in the final triumph of truth and right. The burden of that prophetic messenger is also the message of this hour, commissioned by the time-hallowed law of Israel to marshall us into unknown fields, to lead us upon the untrodden paths of the future.

What is the import of that message? Is it one of gladness and good tidings, or of threatening fear and gloomy forebodings? Will the heavens of our future, now veiled by the sombre clouds of anxiety, open for us the treasures of life, distilling the dew of joy upon our pleasures, and showering the rain of fruitfulness upon our undertakings, or does the twilight of this hour hide the haggard features of want and sorrow, to be but too soon revealed in the lurid glare of harsh reality? No, the

1

5 .

prophecy of this hour sounds a sweeter strain, it echoes a more heavenly melody than the wearisome theme of pleasure and pain, joy and sorrow. Life and death are of God's ordaining; happiness or misfortune often the result of our own doing or misdoing. Should we dread the rulings of Infinite Wisdom and Eternal Goodness? Or shall we tremble before the shadows of our unborn actions? Not our own petty wishes or supercilious fears, but a higher revelation of love, a divine *message of peace* is this hour's assuring promise. Not a prediction, but an illumination from within, shall this beginning of a new time be to us, disclosing to the eye of the soul the richer life, the purer joy, the unfading hope, which we in the blinding chase after the transitory goods of this world often fail to see.

The wisdom of our sages rightly interpreted the true mission of the stern prophet of old, whose name is in later Israel interwoven with every festive occasion and joyous happening. Not to settle by the sword of his authority the partisan strifes and the theological bickerings of the times shall Elijah come again, but only to make peace in the world. Nor are we left in doubt as to the nature of that peace. The last in the line of the inspired Seers of Israel, forecasting the vision of a better humanity, assigns to the austere Gileadite the mission of forerunner and preparer of the great Judgment Day; but not to punish the estranged as on the day of Carmel, but to unite those who have been separated, shall be his duty. In the words of Malachi: "To turn the heart of the fathers to their children, and the heart of the children to their fathers." Let us, then, listen to the voice speaking to us across the gulf of centuries; and find in the heroic *epos* of Elijah the suggestive themes for the festive meditations on this New Year's Day and the Day of Atonement.

I.

"To turn the heart of the fathers to the children." This is the first promise of the prophetic message of this hour.

1. No one who has any capacity for reading the signs of the times can fail to notice the radical changes which have been and are still going

6

on in the opinions of men as to their social, moral and religious relation-
ships. While every age may be called a time of transition, ours is one
of rapid movement and continual surprises. Everywhere the old order is
changing, giving way to the new. And the fact cannot be disguised
that the tendency of this new order has been, and largely still is, one of
destructiveness rather than of reconciliation. This century, now on its
wane, was born amidst the clash of arms and the thunder of cannons,
announcing in most distinct tones that the reign of despotism was over,
and that human right must be re-enthroned. And since that time the
nations have been at work re-arranging the distorted relations of men
to one another. Tyranny and abject servility are being replaced by
popular governments; slavery and serfdom have been swept away by
the reign of free labor. Commerce and industry have broken down the
barriers that divided men and nations, and have given to the restless
activity of man new scope and new direction. But such rapid move-
ments cannot go on without unsettling many a firm foundation of the
social structure. Fiercer than ever rages the struggle of existence; instead of master and slave it is capital and labor wrangling for supremacy. Will this death-struggle end in mutual destruction, or is it the
forerunner of a better time, a better social order, based not upon the
cut-throat competition of unorganized industries, nor upon the unscru-
pulous greed of monopolies and trusts, but upon the righteous and
peaceful adjustment of human labor and human ingenuity? It is cer-
tainly no glory for any one to chuckle over the victory over a number of
men liable to be crushed between the cars, or to rejoice over the fabu-
lous dividends gladdening the hearts of an idle aristocracy, or feeding
a speculative parasitism. To them, and to all like them, who misinterpret
the signs of the times, the grim prophet of Israel predicts years of drought
and barreness, with no smiling heaven of social peace, refreshing with
the dew of happiness the languishing fields of human enterprise. The
Messiah of the better time cannot come, says an ancient tradition, until
Elijah shall first have brought his message to the world ; and this
message is, not to destroy in the bitterness of combat, but to reconcile
the Old with the New, to establish social peace on the basis of human
dignity, justice and love.

7

2. And even so, morally, the **new** time holds diverging tendencies, hiding fatal dangers to the higher life of humanity. The old foundations of **morality have been undermined by the** current of the new science and the spread of an utilitarian theory of ethics changing the vantange ground of **man's motives, duties** and responsibilities. Right and wrong, good and evil, have shifted their meaning; the sanctions of time-honored institutions are questioned, and the individual is left to drift between the stagnant waters of selfishness and the changing quicksands of public opinion. Can we expect the beauteous flowers of **domestic joy and stainless purity,** of self-sacrificing love and lofty idealism to grow and blossom in this time of unrest and moral disturbance? Morality is no invention of the speculative genius, to be adjusted to every passing need; virtue is no experimental theory, to be displaced whenever a new formula is offered. This hour emphasizes the stern fact that, from whatever source our moral nature may be derived — whether it be inspiration or evolution—the law of virtue is an immovable rock, against which the whims, greeds and passions of the individual dash in senseless impotence. This firm conviction was the strong foundation of the moral life of our fathers; this the secret of Israel's indestructibility. Not because their minds harbored the larger truth, but because their hearts cherished a purer ideal of domestic sanctity, and their soul was thrilled by the august sense of moral responsibility, could they survive the changes of time and the destructive sweeps of human hatred and persecution. The new morality, making simple pleasure and pain the motives of life, and individual happiness the ultimate ideal, withdraws from man every stay and support, cuts asunder the invisible ties which connect the present with the past and make the living generation the heir to all glories and achievements of by-gone ages. To reconcile the virtue of the past to the wisdom of the present, to turn the *heart* of the fathers to their children, is the meaning of the prophetic message of this hour. There is no other cure for the ills and woes of modern life, but in the moral rejuvenation of the *home*, that fostering place of all virtue, nobility of character and lofty aspirations.

Fathers and mothers, who to-night pray for the life and happiness

8

of your children, a holier charge is laid on your soul than all fervid supplications; see to it that the sanctuaries of your hearts are wide open to the moral needs of your sons and daughters; that in you and through you they may learn to revere the higher sanctities, and to love the purer joys that lie in the obedience to the moral law. There are no two editions of ethics, one for you, another for your children—one for the old, another for the new generation. It has always been the pride of Israel that a richer feeling of inter-dependence, a deeper sense of love, reverence and gratitude, mark our parental and filial relations. Let this hour be one of holy reunion of hearts that may have grown callous and indifferent; let noble resolves for each other's true welfare crown this natal hour of the year ; let the sacred ties of family affection hold in sweet embrace those who need each other's love and friendship for strength and for guidance to a better, a happier life.

3. And more than that. Let this hour also be a reunion of minds, reconciling the faith of the fathers with the faith of the children. It can not be denied that a fatal split runs through all the issues of our spiritual life, that the edifice of religion is cracked to its very foundations. The new spirit of inquiry and criticism has questioned the authority by which religion claims its title of leadership; it has examined the records and declared them to be human fabrications, instead of divine, infallible truth; it has consigned the Biblical version of creation, of man's origin and early history, to the curiosity chamber of childish guesses and confused notions of the dawning intellect; it has scaled the heavens and pushed the old firmament into infinite space and caused the splendor of the celestial court to fade before the brightness of human reason.

To the influence of such changes in the intellectual position of mankind, the Jewish mind is as amenable as the mind of any other class of people, nay, it is perhaps more disposed to be affected by them than others; for, aside from these general currents of modern thought, our career is beset by special historical and racial difficulties. The older generation, though they may, perhaps, in theory profess the contrary, still hold fast to a form of faith which the younger have outgrown; they still cling to notions of special selection and inherent excellence of descent,

9

which those, cradled in the sunlight of a universal humanity, cannot share, can hardly understand; they still look back upon the glory of the past as the one and chiefest end of Israel's mission, instead of listening to the pulse-beat of modern time, and making the inspiration of the past the throbbing life-blood of the present day and a prophecy of still greater glory yet to come. No wonder that the fresher life and the unspent vigor of our young are not attracted by the spiritual stagnation of Judaism. Deplore as we may this intellectual disunion, we cannot turn back the advancing tide; we cannot reduce the larger thought, the wider sweep of the new time to the narrower circle and the retrospective vision of the older generation. If the new year and the new time is to bring new intellectual life and health, spiritual activity into the religious system of Israel, then this hour must be the harbinger of the spirit of Elijah, the spirit of a higher faith, that will turn the heart of the *fathers* to their children, and teach them the divine duty of love, which conquers while it yields. Let not, by our indifference or stubborness, the heaven of true religion be closed over the hearts of our sons and daughters, so that no refreshing dew of faith and reverence, and no quickening rain of hope and spiritual guidance, descend upon their languishing souls; but let this hour be the beginning of a richer, deeper, higher life, blending the poetry of the past with the music of the present, reconciling the imperishable truths from of old with the larger thought of to-day; turning, indeed, the heart of the fathers to their children.

II.

But this twilight hour is charged with still greater significance; it shall also "turn the heart of the children to their fathers."

1. That this age is in advance of all former ages in social problems, moral endeavors and intellectual achievements, is simply because all those ages of toil and sorrow have preceded it; because all the generations past have been stepping-stones to the present; their wisdom and their follies, their truths and their errors, their loves and their hatreds, have nurtured the soil for the luxuriant growth of modern civilization.

We are children of the past. As our features have semblance to those from whom bodily we are descended, so all our institutions, systems and methods, are the direct continuations of the life-long labor of untold generations; and history is but revelation of the continually unfolding and developing humanity; and time a mirror, reflecting both the grosser and finer features, the light and the shade of the same picture of life.

2. He, therefore, who is impatient with the present and would build for the future, must learn to look with reverence upon the past, and humbly listen to the voice speaking through events and successions, through systems and methods, which have inspired, propelled, strengthened and guided the patient toilers of the past. In architecture and art, in rhetoric and philosophy, in law and administration, we are still the disciples of the great Masters of old; should we not draw inspiration and encouragement also from the treasury of those thoughts and experiences which reveal the higher and holier life of man? Have our fathers lived in vain, thought in vain, suffered in vain, and built up the great structures of moral and spiritual humanity in vain, for their children's children? If the advance of knowledge and the widening of our perspective enable us to see that much which they cherished is illusory, can we dispense with the deeper experience and the clearer insight of their prophetic souls, giving to mankind its true position, its dignity, its goal? And if, in the persons of our own fathers and mothers, we see living representatives of that faithfulness and trust, that loving obedience to the higher law and devotion to a divine idea, characterizing the life of Israel, must we not, in a spirit of humanity that is born of greater wisdom, bend in reverence before their faith, enlarging with childlike piety the narrower meaning of their symbols, and reconciling our truth to their truth?

3. This prophetic appeal to our filial duty finds to-night a responsive echo in our hearts. The festival we celebrate is termed in our prayers "Day of Remembrance."

They to whom God has granted the joy to live in happy communion with their parents, remember with gratitude the treasures of bodily and spiritual blessings they have received from them; and those upon

11

whose path has fallen the shadow of death, remember in this hour the loving care, the tender solicitude of the sainted lives that have gone before them. The noble, manly features of father, brother, or husband, the beauteous form of mother, wife, sister, or daughter—they are before us now—through our tear-bedewed eyes we see them all, and are re-united with them in this hour, welcoming a new year; and in the solemn and grateful memory of their lives, we learn to honor and revere their faith and renew our allegiance to the God of our fathers. Happy those whom their sorrows have made richer in soul; they who sow in tears, in joy shall they reap. Thrice happy those who are privileged to look into the eyes of their beloved ones and there read the meaning of their wishes and hopes, trust and prayers. For them this hour holds a sweeter promise than immunity from sorrow and pain; it comes to ful-fil the prophetic mission "to turn the heart of the children to their fathers."

Thus we greet thee, with cheerful trust, new-born Year, prophet of a new time! Thy features forebode no evil tidings; thy message is one of peace, thy promise reconciliation. Over and above the confused noises of struggling mankind we hear the triumphant song of human right and human love, and our eyes behold the lovely forms of Purity and Happiness, Wisdom and Faith, rising in ever clearer outlines on the heaven of humanity. Yea, that promise will be fulfilled; the spirit of Elijah will come again, and, as in this solemn hour, so in all issues and conflicts of life and belief, "he will turn the heart of the fathers to their children and the heart of the children to their fathers!"

> " Welcome from God, O glad new year!
> Thy paths all yet untrod,
> But prophecy and promise all
> O' glad new year of God ! "

Amen.

THE GIFTS OF LIFE.

NEW YEAR'S MORNING.

Text: I Kings, xvii, 2 14.—"And the word of the Lord came to him, saying, Get thee hence, and turn thee eastward, and hide thyself in the valley of the Cherith, that is before (or on the east side of) the Jordan. And it shall be, thou shalt drink of the brook; and I have commanded the ravens to feed thee there. And it came to pass at last, that the brook dried up, because there had been no heavy rain in the land. And the word of the Lord came to him, saying, Arise, get thee to Zarephath (or Sarepta), which belongeth to Sidon, and dwell there; behold, I have commanded a widow woman there to feed thee. So he arose and went to Zarephath. And when he came to the entrance of the city, behold. a widow woman was there gathering sticks. And he called to her and said, Fetch me, I pray thee, a little water in a vessel, that I may drink. And as she was going to fetch it, he called to her, and said, Bring me, I pray thee, a morsel of bread in thy hand. And she said, As the Lord thy God liveth, I have not a cake, but a handful of meal in a pitcher, and a little oil in a cruse; and behold, I am gathering two sticks, that I may go in and dress it for me and my son, that we may eat it and die. And Elijah said to her, Fear not; go and do as thou hast said; but make me thereof a little cake first, and bring it out to me, and afterwards make for thee and for thy son. For thus saith the Lord the God of Israel, The pitcher of meal shall not be finished, neither shall the cruse of oil fail, until the day that the Lord sendeth heavy rain upon the face of the earth. And she went and did according to the saying of Elijah; and she, and he, and her house, did eat for many days. And the pitcher of meal was not finished, neither did the cruse of oil fail, according to the word of God, which he spake by the hand of Elijah."

Not while winter's icy breath sweeps over snow-shrouded fields and nature lies motionless as in death-like slumber, but when the earth is teeming with life and the kindly soil rewards with unstinted gifts the patient labor of man, does Israel celebrate with prayer and song the birth of a new year. *Life*, not death, is the central thought of Israel's faith; life with its joys and cares, its pleasures and sorrows, its toil and peace, all the thousandfold gifts of the changing seasons, is the song of this first day of the new year. We look back upon the time that lies

2

13

behind us, and we are astonished at finding it so brief, so fleeting, as if it were but yesterday we entered upon our career. How rapidly do the events and experiences of the past flit across the horizon of our memory! The dim vision of childhood vanishes before the brighter image of early youth and the sunny days of strength and vigor and hope. However rich and eventful our later years may have been, again and again our thoughts revert to that period of our life, when, as we stood amidst the scenery of nature, we thought her beauties of earth and sky were but the frame for the picture of ourselves, and life seemed a flowing stream of plenty, inviting us to fill our cup with its limpid waters and quench our thirst for the unknown pleasures of the world. What strange enchantment then hovered over wood and glen, hill and dale! The very air seemed to breathe happiness and joy, and in the friendly sky we saw floating lustrous clouds, images of our hopes and dreams! And yet, no dreams; for reality was fairer than all fancy could portray. How sweet the delight of increasing knowledge; how proud the feeling of self-acquired possession; how glorious the sense of victory over the first obstructions on our path! In the struggle of existence we proved our strength, changing the dark, cruel powers of our desires, appetites and wants into beneficent messengers of our will to win for us our daily bread. As in the quaint poem of Elijah, God commanded the ravens, the most cruel and voracious of winged creatures, to bring to the prophet twice daily bread and meat,—so in our youth and early manhood, the cruel and destructive forces of nature, and the dark powers of human greed and selfishness, are turned as by divine command into agencies of our sustenance, into means for our welfare.

But a change comes over the scene of life. The freshness and buoyancy of youth evaporate like a mist, the vigor and energy of early manhood vanish and dry up like a feeble brook in the summer's drouth; the heavens look empty, the earth barren, and the hungry ravens of cruel want and black care are gathering over our heads, or follow our weary footprints, while we wander in quest of food and drink. Thus, life appears to us in the perspective of riper days. A lonely pilgrimage from the happy streams of youth, through the sorrowful disen-

14

chantment of manhood, to the emptiness of age and the dreary prospect of the grave.

But is this vision a correct picture of life? Compressed between the border lines of a few years, is man's existence on earth but a brief dream and a long, weary struggle, to end in death? Is it then worth while to live at all, to continue this pilgrimage to the bitter end?

The wonderful legend of the ancient Seer of Israel, to whose cheerful message of peace we listened yester eve, holds, under the thin disguise of story and miracle, the true answer to the questions which this day suggests; and in his blessing to the poor widow at whose door he begged for a refreshing drink of water and a morsel of bread, assuring her that for the sake of that gift the pitcher of meal shall not be finished, neither shall the cruse of oil fail, we hear the divine promise of a higher compensation for life's toil than weariness and death; we read the deeper meaning of this day's lesson of the fleetness of time. As yesterday, in the twilight of the natal hour of the new year, the prophet brought to us the first message of peace and reconcilation, so to-day, in the bright sunshine of this morning, he comes to us with his second message of hope and consolation, as never failing gifts of God.

1. The popular philosophy of to-day finds a grim satisfaction in holding up to the gaze of man the sad picture of life, and pointing out all the darker features which add gloom to ugliness. Life, it tells us, is not a dream, but an awful reality. Nature is not the beneficent goddess, inviting us to her feast; a cruel sorceress is she, deceiving us by her arts, until she has made us her dupe, to carry out her designs. She lures us with the promise of pleasure, with the hope of happiness, but she casts us aside as worthless rubbish as soon as we reach out for her dainties. Behind her smiling countenance are hidden the ghastly features of cruelty, destructiveness and death. Look how pitilessly the strife is carried on in the animal world, the strong feeding upon the weak; myriads of sentient beings cast into existence merely to be a prey to the murderous tooth of the pursuer. The higher we rise in the scale of life the more accentuated is this struggle of existence, until in man it reaches its most pronounced type, borrowing weapons of destruction

and cruelty **from** the higher kingdom **of the mind. But** inseparably connected with struggle is pain and suffering. **If the end** of **life is** happiness, pleasure, enjoyment, then existence is a miserable failure, for the **pain** by far outbalances all **pleasures;** the sorrows of life are more numerous than its **joys,** the **moments of happiness** rarer than the long hours **and** days of grief and suffering.

2. From the lower sphere of natural life, man carries the **struggle of existence with all its** attending **suffering** into the **higher realms of social life. And here the** question, as **to the value of existence, assumes a moral aspect. The cynic's answer is: Life is not only a misfortune, it is a positive evil; it lacks the prepondering element of goodness; it is** · **devoid of** that **higher purpose which dreamy sentimentalists would ascribe to it,** and **which, if true, would make it worthy of pursuit. But a glance upon** human **society convinces the impartial observer that wisdom and virtue are the exception, stupidity and meanness the rule. Selfishness, envy and vanity are the** motives in the lives **of most men, fear and hope the** pole-stars **of their** morality. With some, **inherent** wickedness **is** joined **to** greater cunning; they **are** the **beasts of prey,** feeding upon the stupidity of the unwary. Purity, **honesty, self-sacrifice** are virtues publicly admired but not followed, **perhaps secretly sneered at,** as the characteristics of vainglorious saints **or infatuated visionaries.** "The majority **are bad,"** is an **old cry of pessimistic philosophers, repeated in every age, but especially** emphasized **to-day by** the **lurid illustrations** of modern literature, **priding itself upon the nudeness of its** realism. If **the** lives of the **majority be such as depicted by the latest** novel of the fashionable *Russian,* then **human life is not worthy of existence; then** all the embellishments **of** culture,— **the arts that refine, the** melody that stirs the soul, the poetry and philosophy **that uplift the mind, — are but** vile hirelings, pandering to the lower or the higher passions of man; then all social life is a subversion of naturalness, simplicity, and truth, --**all** is semblance, deception, falsehood, as one of the most vehement critics of his time has pithily stated " We possess honor **without virtue,** knowledge **without** wisdom, and pleasure without happiness."

3. Nor **is** the **outlook** of life more cheering if measured by **the**

intellectual standard. How small is the sum of accumulated knowledge in comparison with the unlimited range of the unknown and unknowable! How wearisome and slow the march of the sluggish intellect ! From the first stupid glance at the brilliant sky to the latest interrogations of science, how much fruitless labor, how much wasted energy, how many childish guesses, how many fatal errors, not yet wholly overcome by the riper mind, lie scattered upon the path of humanity, like the bleached bones from numerous caravans lining the trackless wilds of Africa. There they rise in fantastic and grotesque forms like the shapeless and shifting clouds of the starless sky, the systems of old, the cosmogonies and theogonies of the ancients ; the philosophical theories of later schools ; the ideals of the barbarous, self-torturing Middle Ages ; the Utopias of reawakened learning; the maddening search for nature's mysteries; and the new formulas of scientific hypothesis, claiming to possess the keys of heaven and earth, unlocking all secrets of infinite space and the twofold flight of time, backwards and forwards. And yet, with all our vaunted wisdom, what do we *know ?* What things are absolutely established ? Perhaps to-morrow a new theory might disprove all our sifted information, and throw us back upon the traces which we traversed. Once, humanity was as absolutely sure of the truth of the Ptolemean astronomy and the Aristotelean philosophy as we are to-day of the law of gravitation and the potency of evolution. What guaranty have we that these are the final words of scientific discovery ? And, granting even that mankind's intellectual labors are not futile attempts, not meaningless efforts, but successive stages of progress; that knowledge is increasing in spite of this prodigious waste of mental energy, what is the practical outcome of this knowledge ? Does it increase the sum total of human happiness? If it has multiplied our comforts, has it not also multiplied our wants and sharpened our sensibilities. deepening our cares and giving a keener edge to the increasing sorrows of life ? Where are the pangs of disappointment, the misery of want, the agony of dishonor, more deeply felt than by those whose trained intellect lays them open to every influence of civilization ? If the larger knowledge has given us a clearer insight into the methods of nature, has it not thereby robbed us of so much that was dear, and holy, and comforting to the heart? Whence do we come? Whither do we go? These are questions that urgently demand reply. The latest wisdom answers with the oldest cynic: "We came from the dust and we go to the dust, and pre-eminence of man over the beast is not, for all is vanity;" we are linked to the brute below and we go to the grave beneath us. Let us not deceive ourselves by the poet's oft cited wisdom—"And the individual withers that the world be more and more;" for in the light of this wisdom we read of the inevitable doom that awaits the dwellers on earth as our whole planetary system. As it has begun in time so will it end; one after another of the bright orbs will sink into the sun, and all wisdom and all virtue, the moral grandeur and the intellectual splendors of humanity, will be dissolved into the fire-mist of the new world-conflagration. How dreary the outlook, how vain the hope, how cheerless the consolation of humanity! Better not to be, than to live this aimless life! This, in brief, is the sum of that philosophy which claims to stand upon the shoulders of all preceding systems.

4. Are these arguments as to the misery, worthlessness and futility of existence false? Is the picture thus drawn of human life untrue to reality? No, not false, not untrue, but one-sided, and therefore incomplete. There is wanting that one and chiefest element of it all, that element of *light* which alone will account for the presence of the deeper shadows; it is the element of *Religion*. Without it mankind, with all its intellectual life, may indeed be likened to that poor widow with her only child, gathering a few sticks to prepare the last meal and then die. What matters it how long or short the time allotted to man on earth, how slow or swift the years come and go and the seasons change in endless succession! The tide of time brings no promise of compensation; the changing seasons hold out no hope for future happiness; they but repeat the monotonous plaint of the perishableness of all things. One meal more or less, one pleasure more or less, then all is night and unutterable gloom. Religion, like the prophet Elijah in our story, comes to mankind in the humble garb of a suppliant, begging for a gift to sustain its life in this universal drought and famine, this moral and

intellectual despair; but its **very** demand includes the promise of true blessing. "**Prepare** first the meal for me, then think of thyself and thy son, for as the Lord liveth, the meal in the pitcher shall not cease, the oil in the cruse shall not fail, until **the** time when **the Lord** shall give rain unto the land."

Meal and *oil* are the symbols of human enjoyments, bodily **as well as spiritual**; the meal **that nourishes** and sustains, **and the oil that** gladdens and enlightens; they typify the whole range of earthly goods, **the** objects of all the longings, desires, and yearnings of the human **heart,** for the **possession** of which the **race of man** has been wrestling, **struggling, shedding its blood upon every battle-field, hoping** to find in them **and** through them the **soul's peace** and happiness, only to find after thousands of years of strife and suffering that they **are not** worth striving **for.** And this sad experience of the human race is repeated in the life of the individual. When the few years of his youth, with their greater susceptibility and seemingly inexhaustible fountains of enjoyment, are passed, when one after another of **the** sweet illusions that lent special charm to life have dissolved into mist, and cold, sober common sense beholds the realities of life, how much is there left in his estimation of the goods of this world worth striving for? In none of the things that once seemed part of himself has he found lasting peace and happiness. **Driven by** the hungry **desire** from pleasure **to** pleasure, from enjoyment **to enjoyment,** he finds at **last** his life wasted in a profitless chase, and a bitter feeling **of** discontent gnaws at his **soul,** a sense of disgust with **life** fills his heart; or, **if his be the** cynic's temperament, the melancholy mood will give room to the **sneer of** disdain and the sarcasm of contempt. To save himself from the **misery** of life's disgust, or from the irony of his self-contempt, man has in **every** age sought refuge and protection. Old heathenism and **its** modern devotee say: Drain the cup of life to its **dregs, then** fling it away; **eat and** drink, for to-morrow thou shalt die, **when the** last remnant **is consumed.** Buddhism answers: Pleasure is the cause of pain, desire the **source** of **sorrow;** therefore renounce pleasure, kill desire, abnegate the joy **of life, flee** from its allurements, and thou shalt be **free** from the horrors of **existence.** Christianity modulates

19

these strains: Sacrifice the body for the soul, mortify the flesh, deny this world with all its pleasures, and thou wilt purchase thereby everlasting joy in the heaven above. Nor is the stoic's answer more consoling: Pain is the inseparable companion of pleasure; enjoy the one, endure the other. Be not a coward; what thou canst not alter, bear, and if the burden be too heavy, give up thy charge, wrap thy mantle around thee and lie down to eternal sleep. However various these answers, in one point they all agree: Life is a fleeting show; it holds no abiding happiness for man; for his ills and woes, for his sufferings and sorrows, for all the unfulfilled longings of his soul, there is but *one* remedy — its name is *death*.

What answer did Israel voice through the mouth of its prophets? Not *death*, but *life*, not destruction, but devotion, is the solution of the problem of human existence. The magic *word* which changes the perspective and lends fullness to our view: *Duty* is its name! The gift which religion demands of humanity is not sacrifice and renunciation, but devotion to duty, sanctification of the world's goods and pleasures to higher aims and purposes. Prepare first this meal for me, says prophetic religion, then prepare for thyself and thy son, and behold, the source of thy earthly pleasures will not fail, the fountain of thy spiritual life will not cease until the time when the dew of a new life, and the fructifying rain of God's eternal love shall descend upon thy mortal existence, and turn death into deathlessness.

5. Your pleasures are indeed shallow and insipid and are soon exhausted, if intended but for yourself and yours; but if of the means you possess, be they much or little, you seek first to feed the hungry, to reach out the gift of love to the needy, the weary, the fainting, ere you think of your own pleasures, you thereby create for yourself inexhaustible blessings. The joy you plant in the heart of others is multiplied a thousandfold in your own heart; the happiness you spread for others opens the fountain of happiness for yourself. Egotism is self-delusion and self-bereavement; love, kindness, helpfulness, are the wonder-working gifts which, while we extend them to others, are making our own souls the vessels of unceasing, never failing happiness. Israel's faith

does not glory in poverty, asceticism, mortification of the natural faculties of man; it rejoices in the gifts of God, which nature at his command produces so abundantly; but it asks in return that these gifts and faculties be first dedicated to the divine purpose of a moral and spiritual life, making them not ends in themselves, but *means* for upbuilding a nobler self than an eating, drinking and enjoying animal, a nobler humanity than a wrestling, struggling mass, engaged in a war of all against all. The goods of this world are the scaffolding within which man shall erect the beautiful edifice of a truly human character, a real personality.

6. Looked at from this point of view, the intellectual labors of man and mankind rise into the higher sphere of divine knowledge. Without the religious idea, nature is blind, cruel, meaningless. Endowed with a divine purpose, the study of nature's laws lifts us up into the presence of that supreme wisdom which holds and directs the world, and its destinies. Then every seeming failure is a step to higher knowledge, every contribution of the God-seeking mind of man a rich source of never failing wisdom. In the light of this thought the individual finds his labor richly compensated in the increasing wealth of humanity, in the growth of freedom, the reign of virtue, the supremacy of reason wedded to love--in the Kingdom of God on earth. And as the individual man is thus made an integral part of the ever rising and unfolding humanity, so the life of humanity becomes an integral part of a large spiritual system, whose beginning and whose goal is the eternal wisdom and love of God. At this limit of human reason man can think only in symbols, and the soul must reach out in faith and trust to that greater knowledge that is born of immortal hope.

7. And even so are the pains of life transformed into perennial springs of consolation at the miraculous touch of religion. "Whom God loveth he chastiseth," holds more than a convenient phrase. As in the world of nature pain is the goad to the self-preservation of organisms, the indicator of danger, the price for the higher development of races; so in the moral world of man is pain the divine method of education, tears the dew drops falling upon the dry soil of selfishness; sorrows

and woes are the showers irrigating the parched ground of **our spiritual life,** causing our better nature to blossom and **bear a** richer harvest than **before.** And when the rude hand of **death** lays hold on what **is** indeed **a part of our** very selves; when the hope of our heart and solace of our **eye is snatched away** from **us, and our** soul is left in unutterable gloom, **refusing to** be comforted, **it is** the miraculous power of religion alone that **can assuage our** pangs and lift us up out of our depths. The poor **mother in our story** of Elijah, weeping over her dead child, and in her **frantic** grief accusing the prophet **of** having caused the death of her only **son, is** a **type of poor,** sorrow-stricken humanity, mourning over its dead; **she is** a type **of every mother and every father who** have laid their treasures **away under the** soil, and **with their** tears bedew the graves of their beloved ones, **and** stand questioning, doubting, accusing the wisdom of Providence. To them, like to the poor widow of old, the prophet Elijah, the spirit of true religion, comes and mildly speaks: "Give me thy son; entrust thy child to my fatherly care; in the presence of God there is **no** death, but eternal life; see, thy son liveth." Yea, behold the wonder which this prophet has wrought in every age, which he is performing before our very eyes, breathing the spirit of faith upon our dead ones as they live **in our** loving memory, in our richer sympathy with sorrows of others, **in all** the sweeter and loftier hopes **of** our soul for **a** better, nobler life.

These hopes will not deceive us ; they are echoes **from** a divine **world.** May the coming year bring us nearer their fulfillment. May we learn to consecrate our lives to higher aims than **the** pursuit of pleasure, and endeavor to fill out the frame-work of our existence with the ideals of duty, **of** love and devotion; striving to enrich the world by our contribution of heart, **and** mind, and soul, and by thus *giving* **our** best, we shall open **for** ourselves the **never** failing sources of **true** happiness. The dark clouds that obscured our sight sink earthward; brighter than ever we behold the visions of life; golden the future lies before us. Let us not fear, but march courageously on the path of time, mingling our songs of faith, and trust, and hope with the immortal hope of humanity. *Amen.*

SEEKING GOD.

SERMON FOR THE EVE OF DAY OF ATONEMENT.

Text: I Kings, xix, 8-13. "And he arose, and did eat and drink, and went on the strength of that food forty days and forty nights unto the mount of God in Horeb. And he came thither to a cave and lodged there. And behold, the word of the Lord came to him, and said to him, What doest thou here, Elijah? And he said, I have been very zealous for the Eternal the God of hosts. For the children of Israel have forsaken thy covenant, thrown down thine altars, and slain thy prophets with the sword; and I only am left; and they seek my life, to take it away. And he said, Go forth, and stand upon the mount before the Lord. And behold, the Lord passed by; and a great and strong wind rent the mountains, and brake in pieces the rocks before the Lord; but the Lord was not in the wind. And after the wind there was an earthquake; but the Lord was not in the earthquake. And after the earthquake there was a fire; but the Lord was not in the fire. And after the fire there was a still small voice. And it was so, when Elijah heard it, he wrapped his face in his mantle, and went out, and stood in the entering in of the cave."

Into the silence and solitude of the desert Elijah retires, seeking there the God of his fathers, whom, in the tumult and turmoil of human strife, he could not discern. Into the silence and solitude of our soul we must retire, if we are to find again the God of truth, whom, in the struggle of life, in the chase after pleasure, in the obscuring clouds of doubt and disbelief, we have lost. Twice we have listened to the cheering and consoling words of the prophet of Gilead, bringing us the message of peace and the assurance of hope. To-night we follow him across the land of Israel, over the dreary wastes of Judah, up to the many-peaked, awe-surrounded Horeb, the Mount of God, waiting with him for the voice of that revelation that shall dispel our darkness and our fears, and open our spiritual eye to the vision of divine truth. The sacred sounds of the past still vibrate in our ears. With that wonderful song on whose wings are borne through the silent air the sighs and sorrows, the prayers and hopes of Israel's by-gone generations, we began this day's solemn

23

services. What tones! What sublime, unearthly melody breathes in those strains, thrilling the heart to its depth, and awakening in us those memories of childhood and youth, which the busy experience of riper years may for a while repress, but can never obliterate.

This quaint Jewish melody, the ancient *Col-Nidre* song, is a faithful interpretation of our heart's unexpressed and inexpressible longing for that for which the mind of man has been searching ever since it has dawned into consciousness. It is the soul's outcry for God! Since the time that man lifted up his eyes to the starry vault above and questioned: Who are these, and who made them all? when he looked upon the earth beneath and saw the wondrous growth of teeming life in its thousandfold forms and colors, and asked: Who gave birth to all these? Since that time, the spirit of man has been wandering through fertile plains and cheerless deserts, along the winding paths of history, ascending the mountains of larger visions and sacred associations, and still, like the prophet of old, is waiting in silence, perhaps in doubt, for a sign of absolute certainty that its search has not been in vain, but that God will reveal himself to the patient and trusting soul.

Into the cave where once a greater and more patient leader had received a true vision of God, Elijah entered. What was he seeking there in the silence of the night? He followed the shining footprints of Moses, the father of all prophets. There, in the mount of revelation, he hoped to receive the sanction to his life's work, his great zeal for the God of his fathers. So every man and every age will believe in the truths which their minds have found, however imperfect their thoughts may be, and then search, and surely find, the confirmation of their convictions and experiences, in the world of nature around them, in the voice of human history behind them, and in the echo of divine consent reflected in the soul's vision from above. To the savage, in constant struggle with the evil forces of nature, the image of God bears the distorted features of cruelty. He bends before the greater power and reverences that mysterious strength that manifests itself to him in fierce wrath and destructiveness. He sees God in the storm that rends the mountains and breaks in pieces the rocks; he finds Him in the earthquake, destroying the habitation of man and beast; he worships Him in the fire, leaping as a thunderbolt from the heaven above and consuming the mighty oak under which he has found shelter. He sees God in nature, because he projects nature and himself into the image of his God. The ages of barbarism believed that they were fighting the battles of God, conquering the earth, and making it a waste, to carry out a divine command. For the honor of God they slaughtered nations and destroyed human welfare; for his glory they burned the heretics and banished disbelievers from the heritage of their fathers. To their minds God was a great king, sending out his armies to execute his sovereign will, to bend the nations under the sceptre of his majesty. History was to them but the records of God's wars to wreak vengeance on his enemies. Every nation has had its God of revenge.

But the mind is not satisfied with its own creations. The riper intellect soon detects their parentage, and disrobes the idols that had usurped the divine throne. Nothing short of absolute truth will still the craving of the soul. In the collective wisdom of the ripest minds men thought to have found this absolute truth, and worshiped it as the final revelation of that Highest Wisdom that shines in the sunbeam and blossoms in the flower, that rules in nature's laws, and communes through the avenues of thought with the God-seeking soul of man. So every nation has had its Holy Writs and its Mounts of Revelation. The speculative genius of man finds in them all but partial truth, fragments of knowledge, all pointing to a still higher truth, which shall satisfy the hunger of the soul. However much human reason will weary itself in the attempt to define the Infinite and invent new names for the Nameless, it is soon left behind by the onward-reaching power of the soul, which yearns for greater truth than all intellectual postulates. For God is not the product of the human mind, not the result of human reasoning. *The soul feels that God is, and that He is the source of all,* and struggles upward to its divine origin. All the experiences of the past, the God of nature, the God of history, the God of revelation, man must first translate into experiences of his soul, ere these ideas and ideals can become truths for him.

25

And so to us, as to the ancient prophet, waiting for the revelation of the highest truth, seeking to find the true nature and essence of God, comes the divine voice: What doest thou here? Here thou wilt not find Me. I am not closed up in the mystery of a past revelation. Go forth, stand upon the mount of a larger vision. The storm, the earthquake and the fire are the ideals of past generations. God is not in them now. Proud mortal, behold, thou canst know nothing outside of thyself. Into thy inmost being turn thine eye, seek there the traces of Him who has made thy soul an image of Himself, and thou wilt discern Him everywhere, in the tempest as well as in the calm that follows it, in the destroying earthquake and in the consuming fire, as well as in the soft and peaceful rustling of the leaves, making sweet music to the play of the sunbeams.

This answer is an echo of another revelation which one, greater than Elijah, had received on Mount Horeb. After all the manifestations of God's power in behalf of Israel; after the exodus from Egypt and the proclamation on Sinai, Moses still desires to see the glory of God. And he is bidden to stand where Elijah stood six hundred years after him, and wait for the glory of God to pass by him. In words that will forever stand as the soul's deepest experience, that divine glory is described there. And the Lord passed by before his countenance, and proclaimed His true name, saying: "The Eternal, the Eternal, is a merciful and gracious God, patient, and abundant in love and truth, keeping kindness unto thousands, forgiving iniquity, transgression and sin, but will by no means clear the guilty." This is not the language of philosophy, it is the language of the heart, the language of human experience. This is the "still small voice," or to give a better translation, the "soft voice of silence," speaking louder than the thundering hurricane, that silence of the inward vision, coming to us after the storm of passion has spent its fury and the fire of misguided imagination has consumed itself.

What is God? God is Eternal Goodness, this the first assurance of the God-seeking soul. Whatever God be to the myriads of worlds rolling in their courses, to man He reveals Himself only through this human side. If you seek to find God, seek Him in the goodness of your heart, in the kindness of which you are susceptible, in the grace which you bestow upon others, in the love which reveals to you the depths of another's soul, in the patience with which you bear the faults and frailties of others, in the mercy of forgiveness to which your heart is moved by the penitent tear of him who has grieved you. What theory can bring home to you the truth that God is the loving father of all men, except that your heart goes out in sympathy to others, and learns to love and honor the human dignity in every man? No theology can convince you that God may forgive your sins, unless you have learned to open your soul in mercy, repressing anger and revenge, and lovingly forgive the sins committed against you. Through this experience of your soul, you touch the springs of that Eternal Goodness, from whose fathomless source human goodness must be derived. There is no other way of reasoning; not backward from God to man, but upward, from man to God. This is the meaning of the Psalmist's seeming paradox, when speaking of the manifestations of God in man : " To the pure Thou wilt show thyself pure, to the merciful Thou wilt show thyself merciful, to the upright man upright, and to crooked Thou wilt show thyself perverse." This was the experience of all the seers and inspired bards of Israel. They found God in their loving soul, therefore they could find Him again in the events of nature and of life, in the history of nations, and in the fate of their people. God's love is eternal and unchanging; man's uncontrolled desires, his hatred and revengefulness, his unloving temper, separates him from God.

And this, too, we find in the deepest recess of the soul: God is Eternal Justice; his righteousness is commensurate with his love. He will by no means clear the guilty. God's love often manifests itself in deeds of justice, in the punishment of wickedness, in the destruction of evil, in the trials of the best and noblest souls. In the lower realm of nature, we have found the law of heredity as the stern decree by which organisms survive or succumb. In the sphere of man, the sins of parents are visited upon the children in the consequences of evil deeds and evil inclinations. Sin carries its punishment along with the deed, and reaches forward into the next generations. Not by any frown on the divine brow, but by the silent working of forces following along the traces of our sins until they have overtaken us and crushed us, are we made to feel that we are amidst eternal and unbending laws which brook no contradiction, and thus arises in us the consciousness of a just and a righteous God, who will not clear the guilty, visiting the sins of the parents upon the children and the children's children to the third generation. And when we are gone astray, when we have torn the crown of human dignity from our head and sunk to the level of brute creation, when we have sought through selfishness and greed, through deception and falsehood, through heartlessness and ingratitude, to gain the better advantage of life—what is it that indicates our wrong-doing, and punishes us for our sins? Is it not that soft voice of silence, the tender voice of conscience, rebuking us for our follies, robbing us of the rest of mind and the peace of the soul? No tribunal can inflict a severer punishment than the tribunal of our conscience in the silence of self-examination. By unimpeachable evidence it proves our guilt; for we ourselves must testify against ourselves; the law by which we are judged needs no interpretation, it is engraved upon our hearts; and the verdict of conscience is severer than death—it is *self-contempt*. Is not that a voice divine, speaking louder than the roaring storm or the rolling thunder? Whence comes to us this soft voice of silence, if not from Him who is Eternal Justice and Love, bearing the universe in His arms, yet choosing to dwell in houses of clay and making the soul of man the temple of his glory? Yea, man's innate sense of justice, his recognition of his shortcomings, his pangs and sorrows and self-inflicted punishment, are the heart's deepest assurance of God's presence.

> Go not, my soul, in search of Him,
>   Thou wilt not find Him there, —
> Or in the depths of shadow dim,
>   Or heights of upper air.
>
> For not in far-off realms of space
>   The Spirit hath its throne;
> In every heart it findeth place
>   And waiteth to be known.

Thought answereth alone to thought,
 And soul with soul hath kin;
The outward God he findeth not
 Who finds not God within.

And if the vision come to thee
 Revealed by inward sign,
Earth will be full of Deity
 And with His glory shine !

Thou shalt not want for company,
 Nor pitch thy tent alone;
The indwelling God will go with thee
 And show thee of His own.

O gift of gifts, O grace of grace,
 That God should condescend
To make thy heart His dwelling place
 And be thy daily Friend !

Then go not thou in search of Him,
 But to thyself repair ;
Wait thou within the silence dim,
 And thou shalt find Him there !

                        —F. L. Hosmer.

·

THE ALTARS REBUILT.

Text: I Kings, xviii, 20-40 (Abridged).—"And Elijah drew nigh unto all the people, and said, How long halt ye between two opinions? If the Eternal be God, follow him; but if Baal, then follow him. And the people answered him not a word. Then said Elijah to the people, I, one only, remain a prophet of the Eternal; but Baal's prophets are four hundred and fifty men. And Elijah said to all the people, Come near to me. And all the people came near to him, and he repaired the altar of the Lord that was broken down. And it came to pass at the time of offering up the meal offering, that Elijah the prophet came near, and said, O Eternal, God of Abraham, of Isaac, and of Israel, let it be known this day, that thou art God in Israel, and that I am thy servant, and that I have done all these things at thy word. Answer me, O Eternal, answer me, that this people may know that thou art God, and do thou turn their heart back again. Then the fire of the Lord fell, and consumed the burnt offering, and the wood, and the stones, and the dust, and licked up the water that was in the trench. And when the people saw it, they fell on their faces: and they said, The Eternal, He is God, the Eternal, He is God."

Were to-day, by some miraculous proceeding, one of the ancient Seers of Israel to come among us, say the austere prophet of Gilead, the fearless and undaunted Elijah, addressing us in his wonted plain, undisguised words, rebuking us for our negligence in matters that concern our holiest interests, threatening us, in the burning anger of his conviction, with dire calamities and utter destruction, or lifting up his tearful voice in prayer to the God of our fathers, imploring him to turn the perverted heart of his children unto Him, or performing before our eyes any of the miracles reported of him in the chronicles of old; what, my friends, do you think, would be the impression produced upon us; what kind of reception would we accord him? I am afraid we would in this respect not be "better than our fathers." We would, perhaps, listen to him, appreciate his good intention, then turn to our wonted occupation and way of thinking. His words, I am bold to say, would not effect a radical change in our opinions, nor leave a lasting impression upon our hearts. Some of us would even raise serious objections to his ministraton.

To a great many, the lean, long, haggard figure of the mountaineer, the dark, piercing look, the coarse, unfashionable habilament, the plain, unpolished speech, would seem decidedly out of date and place in a modern Jewish congregation; badly fitting into the frame of our services and gatherings. The man to conduct our divine worship, and to speak to us the word of God, is not expected to be of the Elijah type; but rather a portly, polite gentleman, not careless even of the smaller duties of dress and gesture, unobtrusive in mien and look, careful and measured in speech as well as in action, knowing his position to be, not a leader of public opinion, not a pathfinder of new ways and methods, but simply a trained orator and skillful expounder of opinions and customs held by those who placed him there, and whose word of wisdom and might — generally the latter — may displace him from his honorable post. No! Elijah would not do at all in a modern Jewish congregation. A man who has the audacity to frown at the king, and to lay the charge of corruption and murder upon his very crown; who, in face of an overwhelming majority of prophets and priests, eating at the king's table and fawning at his majesty, declares that he—Elijah—alone is right; that the word of God in his mouth is *truth*, and that those who obey the king's behest and minister at the new altars of Baal and Astarte are traitors to their God and their people; a man who could speak so disrespectfully of those who differed from him in their religious opinions, and who, in a fit of rage, could slaughter four hundred and fifty prophets of Baal—such a man, and be he the greatest of God's prophets, the most earnest and convincing defender of Israel's faith, could not be elected to the pulpit of the smallest or the most ignorant of our congregations. He could not get so much as a hearing.

In synagogues and churches the name of Elijah is uttered with great reverence, and is associated with many living hopes of the two religious systems. Whether in the literal or spiritual interpretation of the great Messiah's idea, Elijah holds the title of pre-

31

decessor and preparer of the way. In a New Testament vision he appears by the side of Moses; in Jewish tradition, he comes to every family gathered around the festive board on the eve of the Passover, partaking of the cup of wine specially placed at his disposal; he is present whenever a son is introduced into the covenant of his fathers; he often appears to toiling, care-worn men, giving a coin or a key which change whatever they touch into genuine gold, or teaching them a simple word which, uttered at the right time, turns the tears of grief into pearls of happiness. And still, I hold, were this same Elijah to come among us, living, speaking, acting in accordance with his character, he would find himself confronted by the same difficulties which he found in the days of Ahab. No doubt, to the "gentlemen" in Samaria, the wild preacher from Gilead was a most repulsive sight; to their refined taste, his growling, thundering voice was very unsympathetic; his denunciations coarse and untimely. They preferred the smoother eloquence of the royal prophets, and the sweet, enchanting music coming from the lips of Astarte's priestesses. But, friends, we need have no fear that Elijah will ever come to frighten or to fret us with his presence; he will not intrude upon our well-regulated system of worship, nor offend our culture by his rude speech.

Whether Elijah ever lived at all, is a disputable question among scholars; but if he did, he quitted the scene of life over twenty-seven hundred years ago, and is not likely to be in a position for itinerant preaching. Even should we believe in the literal word of the Bible, that Elijah was taken up by a fiery team and in body ascended to heaven, it is not at all probable that, remembering the sad experiences of the past, and foreseeing the poor result of his work among us, he should leave his serene home, and undertake a new journey to the earth. So let us dissuade our minds from any anxiety on that point. Neither Elijah, nor any of the old thundering prophets, will trouble us to-day.

And yet I assure you, though Elijah is dead, and the prophets that lived after him are dead also, *one* prophet is here among us who thinks, and feels, and speaks with the soul of Elijah, *one* who with the courage and fearlessness of the prophets of old, cries to us in accents not to be overheard or misunderstood, appeals to us in words that burn like leaping flames into our souls, chastising us for our sins and follies, and calling us back to our duty to our God and to the religion of our fathers. It is none else than the *Day of Atonement* itself! This day comes to us, indeed, like the prophet Elijah, plain, old fashioned, sombre looking, unyielding, uncompromising. What it tells are not festive congratulations; it is not a day of gladness, but of deep, earnest self-examination. Of all the festivals and sacred days of Israel, this day alone has retained its original character; with Elijah it says: I alone have remained a true prophet of God! It has not yielded to the pressure of the times, and refuses to be "reformed." As a true prophet, it brings its heavenly message of warning to rich and poor, high or low, without fear or favor, and challenges us to a test between the results of true religion and the beguiling influence of make-belief and self-deception. As yet, this prophet has never spoken in vain; year after year it has aroused in us holier feelings and noble resolves, and often has brought us back to our better selves. Let me, to-day, be its interpreter; let me speak to you in plain, earnest, undisguised words of the sins and evils we have committed, let me plead to you in the name of Him, before whom falsehood cannot stand, and deception cannot abide. Oh, that I had the power of Elijah to call down the heavenly fire of true conviction upon the altar of your hearts, that I could shame into silence the false prophets—carelessness, self-complaisance, cowardice, time-serving, greed and stupidity—that step between you and your God to lead you away from the religion of your fathers! Alas, mine is but the weak word, quickly spoken and soon forgotten! And yet I trust that God will bless this word of mine that it shall not return empty, but shall bring to pass that for which it was sent. Oh my God, strenghten me for this work, and take away from my eyes the fear of man, and let thy truth alone and the thought of thy presence guide me in this hour!

1. To the prophets of old religion was not a matter of tradition or conventionality, far less was it to them a matter of business or policy, as it was to the priests or kings. With them religion was the deepest and

33

most conclusive of all convictions, it was *life* itself. God, to their minds, was not a term for an indefinite religious aspiration, but the life of their life, the soul of their soul. Their very occupation and name became to them symbols of their divine mission. *Elijah* means: My God is Jehovah, the Eternal, I know no other. To him I have devoted my life, my powers. This name stands as the type of all prophets of Israel, before and after Elijah. They were all men of thorough-going conviction; their faith in the God of Israel did not rest upon popular assent, but was a direct voice speaking to them through their own consciousness. Such men are always in the minority. The true people of Israel have always been few in number. The masses are not moved by conviction, but by convenience; their God is not Jehovah, the Invisible, the Eternal, whose law is unyielding truth, whose service is uncompromising devotion to duty, whose nature is unchanging love, justice and holiness; but Baal, the visible deity, whose symbol is the sun, now smiling in friendly rays, now hidden behind obscuring clouds, to-day kissing the flowers out of their sleep, to-morrow parching up field and meadow, that all creatures languish for thirst—a type of that idol worshiped at all times by the masses, the idol called: *Public Opinion.* The masses are swayed by the outlook of temporal prosperity; they bend the knee before the success-ful hero ; they praise the victorious conqueror. Let the tide of fate sweep against them, and the loudest praises quickly change into public accusations. He who yesterday knelt in reverence before the child of fortune, will to-day, when the sun of luck no more smiles upon it, be the first to strangle it, if by this act he may win the favor of the new powers that be. Public opinion is no gauge of the worth of a man; it is not the measure of value of principles or institutions; it is no criterion of truth or right. "The voice of the people is the voice of God," is one of those favorite catchwords skillfully employed by demagogues to tickle the long ears of his sovereign majesty—the Public. One man with the con-viction of truth in his heart is a majority, and his voice *is* the voice of God. And when his words fall like thunderbolts upon the torpid souls of the massees, awakening into consciousness whatever there is yet in them that is divine, and thus morally forcing their assent to his convictions, then, and then only, the voice of the people becomes the voice of God.

2. This spiritual fact is the key to the right understanding, not only of the activity of Israel's prophets, but to the great question of the *Mission of Israel.*

What is the meaning and purpose of Israel's existence, what is the position he occupies in the life of the nations, what is his destiny in the larger kingdom of the spiritual life of humanity? The prophets of old, as well as the best and noblest minds of the people, conceived this mission to be at all times a *divine* one. Israel is to be a people of God, that is, his mission is to historically body forth those religious ideas which constitute mankind's true dignity and wealth; developing upon the basis of his national life those laws, institutions, and ideals which have given value and direction to the higher life of humanity. That this was his divinely appointed mission, and not the result of accidental combinations, that Israel did not happily or unhappily blunder into his true vocation, but was purposely led, nay often forced, upon his line of action, is testified by every page of his wonderful history. To many a nation of antiquity the thought of its mission dawned when its history had closed; but Israel's history begins with a clear outline of his divine calling. The true, the ideal Israel, though constituting but a minority of the people, always thought, felt, and acted in the spirit implied in the name, Elijah: "My God is Jehovah; I am sent into this world to proclaim his truth, to preach his holiness, to testify of his righteousness, to spread the knowledge of his justice and love, to teach the nations the fatherhead of God and the brotherhood of man, to build up the kingdom of God on earth."

3. Not so did this mission appear to the majority of the people, their leaders, priests and kings. To them the worldly welfare was the first concern. To be a strong, prosperous nation, to push the border lines of the country far into the neighboring kingdoms ; to build strong cities, stud the mountains with fortresses, and crown the hills with royal palaces and stately temples,— was the ambition of those who, through popular favor, treachery, rebellion, or the massacre of dynasties, held

35

the reins of government. To them the religion of Israel was but a part of the state machinery, and Jehovah, the God of Israel, stood on a par with all other respectable or disrespectable deities of the surrounding heathen nations. To win their favor, and the political alliance of the people who worshiped them, was considered an act of prudence and statescraft. Baal and Jehovah were all the same to them, if but by the change some profit was visible, new conquests, better times, new markets for Israelitish goods, honors at foreign courts; or, to the stupid majority, the outlook for a good harvest or immunity from prevailing sickness.

Against such treachery and faithlessness toward the inmost life of Israel the prophets protested most vehemently, even at the risk of their own lives—and not in vain. Before their thundering voices the thrones of idolatrous kings trembled, and the walls of their palaces sunk into ruins. This inward conflict between the ideal interests of the people and the question of material welfare could end but in the destruction of the Iraelitish commonwealth. Yea, the great zeal of the prophets for the purity of the religion of Israel, for the ideal life of the people, was the direct cause of the total annihilation of the Jewish State. They killed the body that the soul might live. What would have been the fate of the people without these uncompromising upholders of the ideal mission of Israel? If the policy of their kings had obtained, the nation might have existed a few hundred years longer; the princes would have built some more palaces, filled their stables with more horses, their courts with more slaves, their harems with the daughters of many nations; the nobles and grandees would have enjoyed more gorgeous feasts, the priests would have continued for some time longer to slaughter victims, and unctiously sprinkle their blood upon the altars, to swing the censer with grace and dignity, and with well-trained, melodious voice utter the prescribed benediction. Israel's merchants would have carried on much longer a successful and profitable business with Tyre, Sydon, Egypt and Babylon. But the religion of Israel would have been stifled by this material prosperity. The God of hosts would have lost his identity among the host of gods, and Israel would have shared the fate of those very nations whose beliefs, customs and laws they were so eager to accept. Through the loss of his political existence, Israel has saved his *soul alive*, and has become, by the very martyrdom which he had to endure, the Savior, the Messiah, of humanity, the mediator between God and man. *The soul of Israel is his religion*, which, in one form or another, is now the animating spiritual force in the life of the civilized nations of the earth.

4. Nor is this mission of Israel, to be the prophet of true religion, ended in our time, though some of the fundamental principles of his faith have been universally accepted. The last word of Israel has not yet been spoken; Judaism, Christianity, Mohammedanism, are not final truths, but phases of his spiritual life. The religion of humanity, the all-embracing faith of an *Universal Religion* is yet to come, and as of old, Israel is the Elijah, the forerunner and preparer of that great messianic time—out of the soul-life of Israel must that future religion of humanity be born. This is no dream, nor proud self-exultation, nor the vaunt of despair—it is the verdict of history as well as of faith. Of all the nations of antiquity, before and after Israel's appearance in history, none has survived a certain period of time. Within the limits of a few hundred years the proudest and most powerful nations had exhausted their productive genius; they gave their contribution to the wealth of humanity, and then disappeared from the face of the earth. Their mission was ended. New nations sprang up in their stead, to take up the task of humanity, to labor at the solution of some new problems, and to contribute their share to the larger life of mankind. But all along the line of history we see Israel continue his life-work. Deprived of his national independence, twice exiled and robbed of his rights, driven from land to land, and proclaimed an alien wherever he set his weary foot, plundered, tortured, burned, massacred, on account of his faith, Israel could not be destroyed, but still exists, and is to-day as numerous as he has ever been in the days of his kings! What truth does his historical exception teach us? What else, but the divine lesson that Israel's mission is not yet ended, that his presence is still needed as an essential element of humanity?

5. Applying these truths to our own wants and the problem of

to-day, the question comes home to us with **double force:** What are we? If not a *Religious Community,* inspired by the life-mission of Israel, what place do we **hold in** the organic life of modern nations? It is not difficult to find the answer, though it be humiliating to our self-love. Then **there is no room for Israel** on this earth! Then we stand on a level **with the Gypsies or some** other wandering **tribes** who have outlived the mission of their people, and who, in smaller or larger numbers, present the painful spectacle of a degraded **race.** The *irreligious Jew,* the Jewish atheist, is an anomaly, **an** historical self-contradiction. To claim superiority **on the** strength of some **racial differences and distinctions ;** to boast of the keenness of the **Jewish intellect and ability, so gloriously** demonstrated by **the large number of our** successful **merchants, financiers,** artists, statesmen, or **even politicians; to** "point **with pride"—to** borrow a favorite **phrase of our great after-dinner** orators and political aspirants—to the great **men that come from** "our people," gracing the pages of modern history, our **Rothschilds, Bleichroders,** Mocattos and Belmonts; our Disraelis, Cremieaux **and Laskers, our** Mayerbeers, Mendelssohns, **Rubinsteins and Offenbachs, our Rachels,** Davisons, **Barnais** and Sarah Bernhardts—not **to mention the** innumerable host of famous Jewish chess-players, **billiardists, dancers** and ward-politicians—to hold *these* up as the **types of Israel's genius and the flowering** of our millennial **historical career, is a most** sorrowful misinterpretation of the grandest **and holiest mission, of the** noblest and loftiest **purpose that** has ever been conceived **by any** nation on the **earth! All these** worldly achievements may **be very desirable, but** they are of secondary importance. Israel shall not exclude himself from the practical life of the **nations, but shall** remain in close contact with all that concerns the welfare **of the** people with whom **he** shares a common political life; but **his true, his higher mission, is to be** a prophet of God, **to** exemplify in **his domestic** relations, **in his social intercourse,** in his religious associations and intellectual labors, the spirit that animated the prophets of old, the spirit that breathes through the Mosaic legislation, aiming to tone down the harsh distinctions **of wealth and poverty, to** inspire with the fervor of his enthusiasm the moral **endeavor of the age,** to clarify through the purity of his faith, and the unselfish devotion of his life to humanity's highest tasks, the faith of mankind in the One, Eternal God of Israel, the Father of all men.

6. If this be our mission now, as it has ever been in the past, the question which the Day of Atonement puts to us is : "Have you been true to your mission?" And the answer comes back : We have not! We have been true to our material interests, but false to our divine trust. We have striven to accumulate wealth at the cost of our religious and intellectual life. We have sacrificed the soul for the body, the end for the means; we have given God for Baal! From our houses we have banished the faith of our fathers ; with our own hands we have broken down the altars of devotion, and brought our children up in ignorance of Israel's great truths. We have sold our Sabbaths and our holidays, and bartered away the rest of the body and the peace of the mind. To our sons and daughters we have set the example of cold indifference or stupid sneering at the holiest and most venerable forms of our ancestral faith, and now we wonder why the heaven of our spiritual life is closed and the ground of our religious activity is dry and barren ; why our prayers are without devotion, our services without uplifting inspiration ; why our children turn away from our sanctuaries to seek not a truer faith, but the enchanting worship of Baal and Astarte — wealth and pleasure!

If *we* are not true-hearted and sincere in our convictions, if we ourselves are halting between two opinions, how can we call down the heavenly fire of true faith upon the souls of our children? That we may be better able to fulfill our mission, God has endowed us with wonderful faculties and abilities, which have made us proverbial ; he has given us greater vitality, to survive the storms of hatred and persecution ; wealth and wisdom, to emulate in the solution of the greatest problems of mankind. What use have we made of these faculties and endowments? Have our sacrifices in behalf of toiling and suffering humanity, in behalf of the ignorant who are striving for light, the down-trodden who are yearning for liberty, the poverty, misery and vice stalking in our streets — have our sacrifices for all these things been commensurate with our means? What have we done for the honor of Israel, for the strength-

39

ening of our faith, the spreading of our truths, the sanctification of God's name among the nations, that through our actions we may kill the hydra-headed monster of prejudice and race-hatred still prevailing against the descendants of Abraham? Where are the Jewish libraries, high schools, seminaries and universities, established by our Jewish Astors and Vanderbilts? How piteously poor do the few attempts at a larger humanitarian work look in comparison with our wealth and numbers in this country. I mention with due respect the praise-worthy efforts made by collective bodies and by some large-hearted individual men and women — our asylums and hospitals, which must live from hand to mouth, our theological seminary in Cincinnati, which ekes out a precarious existence, the manual training school in this city, the royal charities of *Mr. Jacob Schiff*, of New York, and last, but not least, the blessed work of the "Society for the Education of Jewish Orphans," created by the munificence of *Mrs. Elisa Frank* in our midst, who thereby has set a noble example of the true uses of wealth.

But I ask you, is this sufficient? Should not a city like this possess a *Jewish library*, offering ample information as well as living instruction, in the shape of lecture courses on the most vital questions of Israelitish life? Should not a Jewish community like this provide an institution where our *daughters* may receive as thorough and classical an education as in the best and most fashionable seminaries in the land, with the additional benefit of Jewish religious influence, and not leave the task of moulding the heart and mind of the wives and mothers of the coming generation, to the quiet proselytizing efforts of Catholic and Methodist schools? .

Nor should we overlook the dangers threatening the honor and faith of Israel in connection with the increasing immigration of brethren from lands of barbarism, political misrule, and religious darkness. If Christian associations go to the trouble of establishing missionary schools among them, shall not we, who are of their flesh and blood, take a warmer interest in their moral and intellectual welfare, and by patient toil, by kindly and brotherly treatment, win their confidence, their implicit trust, and raise them up to that level of American citizenship on which we stand?

7. Yes, ignorance, intellectual and spiritual torpitude, is the evil which besets modern Israel; the Baal against whom we must fight with the weapons of the ancient prophets, with the weapons of the spirit, the weapons of truth, sincerity and faithfulness to principle. Step up to your duty, ye leaders in Israel, you fathers and mothers, build up the altar of your faith, put the fragments of the religion of your childhood together, and place upon the rebuilt altar the sacrifice of your devotion, your love, and see whether the true God of our fathers will not accept your offerings and respond with the heavenly flame of enthusiasm kindling the hearts of our children for the higher, the deviner life of Israel! Witness the miracle which sincere faith can perform before our eyes. If this Day is a true prophet of God it will not leave us ere we shall have decided for ourselves whether we shall serve Adonay, the God of our fathers, the God of truth, and right, and duty, or whether we shall continue to follow Baal, the idol of selfishness, pleasure, mental and moral indolence, pride, ignorance and stubborness. Behold, long enough have we prayed to our idols to open for us the heaven of happiness and to shower upon us the blessing of true religion. Long enough have we followed after every fashion and worshiped at the altars of every new theory: Atheism, materialism, agnosticism—they have not responded to our call, they have not answered the soul's cry for the God of truth. But now, this day comes near to us, like the prophet Elijah to misguided Israel of old, and with the words of his prayer it thrills our souls with awe and reverence. In tones that will forever ring through the ages, piercing the ears of indifference and arousing the hearts of the faithless to their duty, it cries: "O Eternal, God of Abraham, Isaac and Israel, let it be known this day that thou art God in Israel, and that I am thy servant, and that I have done all those things at Thy word. Answer me, O Eternal, answer me, that this people may know, that thou Adonay art God, and do thou turn their heart back again!" Touched by the spark of faith, rekindled by the heavenly fire, we cry out with penitent Israel of old, even as we shall once utter with our last breath: "Adonay ha-Elohim—The Eternal, he is God; the Eternal he is God!" With this prayer and with this answer we dedicate and consecrate ourselves anew to the service of the God of our fathers, to the divine mission of Israel, to be the Elijah of humanity.

Amen.

www.ingramcontent.com/pod-product-compliance
Lightning Source LLC
Chambersburg PA
CBHW021444090426
42739CB00009B/1642